WHAT TO KNOW BEFORE YOU GO

WHAT TO KNOW
BEFORE YOU GO

AN INSIDER'S HONEST ANSWERS
TO THE MOST COMMONLY ASKED QUESTIONS ABOUT
DEATH, GRIEF, AND FUNERALS

BY SCOTT MUELLER

EDITED BY TAELOR JOHNSON

AND PAMELA TRAPHAGEN

Published by Mueller Memorial Inc.
835 Johnson Pkwy
St Paul MN 55106

Readers should be aware that Internet web sites offered as sources for further information may have changed or disappeared between the time this was written and when it was read.

Mueller, Scott, 1958-
What to know before you go: An insider's answers to the most commonly asked questions about death, grief, and funerals

ISBN: 978-0-9885500-0-1
Second Edition
Printed in the United States of America

DEDICATION

Taking care of my neighbors, friends, and relatives when a death touches their lives helps me live mine. Most of the time, death comes as expected at the end of a long life, but sometimes it marks the end of a life tragically cut short. As a witness to this, I consider the life of the person and not the death itself.

This profession has been a gift to me. Every day I am reminded how short this life can be and this is a good time to be grateful.

First to my parents, Al and Connie Mueller, who started a business based on compassion and built it with integrity.

To my loving wife, Heidi, who understands my commitment and supports the long and unscheduled hours it requires.

To my employees, whose commitment allows me to be involved in my community.

To my grandchildren, Summer, Charlie, and Siri, who replenish my spirit.

And to my daughter, Taelor Johnson, who acts as my collaborator, editor, and motivator. Without her, this project would still be an idea.

Scott

CONTENTS

INTRODUCTION

I'm sure you'd rather be reading a book about exotic Morocco, tying the perfect fly lure, a torrid romance, or just about anything other than the exciting topic of funerals. Yet here you are, making the good decisions, putting in the time, and trying to be prepared.

It's no small feat to conclude that you need more information about the services needed at the time of death, because such a conclusion usually means that you're either planning for your death or the death of someone you love. That's a weighty realization, my friend, and you surely deserve some praise for facing this difficult reality and picking up this book to get expert answers to tough questions.

I grew up around my family's funeral home and joined my dad in the funeral profession nearly four decades ago. My dad, Al Mueller, was a widely respected and beloved guy in our community and he really set the standard for what I wanted to be as an intern, then a director, and ultimately an owner. And I can tell you, Dad's standard was set mighty high.

It's because of my father, and my desire to continue his legacy, that Mueller Memorial has become locally trusted and nationally recognized. Our reputation and a commitment to service has afforded me the opportunity to become highly involved in research, serving national funeral service organizations, and giving presentations on professional development. However, all of those things are secondary to the privilege of being someone who my neighbors and friends can lean on. It is my honor to be given the opportunity to help them through some of the most difficult and confusing times of their lives.

I wrote this book is to help you understand your options and make informed decisions about how to honor wishes, celebrate the life lived, and frame the way friends and family begin the grief process. These decisions carry a lot of responsibility — and a lot of questions. In my years as a funeral director, I have found that I tend to be asked a certain set of common questions. This book answers those questions in the most honest and practical way possible. In order to do that, I will be dispensing with some of the words commonly used at the time of a death: passed away, loved one, and departed. Those words are generally used to avoid the use of the "D" words: death, dead, died, and dies. In many circumstances, "D" words can come off as sounding incredibly harsh and it's not my intention to sound insensitive. It is my intention to answer the questions in a way that is honest, concise, and informative. This places our conversation somewhere between the way in which I speak to the people we serve and the way I speak to my colleagues.

It is my sincere hope that you'll be able to use this book, and my lifetime of experience being involved in and around funerals, to help you create a valuable, memorable, meaningful, and maybe even a fun memorial for yourself or someone you love; and that you can accomplish this while feeling informed, in charge, empowered, and respected. Death is a time of emotional vulnerability, but that doesn't have to mean that you will be taken advantage of. It just means that you need to work with people you like and trust: people who truly have your best interests at heart and can guide you toward realizing your vision of what you want the memorial to be, while sharing valuable insights that will help to make the events go smoothly and in the most meaningful way possible.

Trust is often hard to come by if you're not acquainted with your funeral director, but there is no reason why this needs to be true. If you take steps to find a funeral service provider that you connect with or one who simply makes you feel comfortable, you'll find that person can carry a lot of your burden with precious phrases such as: "It's taken care of," "No problem," or "We've got this covered." If you can put aside the stereotypical images and ideas of what funeral directors are, then you can be open to looking at them as personal concierges for your wonderful memorial and see them as your guide for what is a once-in-a-lifetime event.

Section One

Why You Don't Trust Me

QUESTION ONE

HOW DO I KEEP FROM BEING RIPPED OFF?

Many people have a distrusting attitude towards funeral directors and funeral homes because of the stereotype that's been imparted over the years. This stereotype has been created and reinforced by film and television media, by people who have written books that are critical of the profession, and by news reports of the very few funeral homes that participate in criminal activity.

The film and television version of a funeral director probably rings true with what you might feel already. The funeral director stereotype is a person who is over six feet tall. He's thin, he's lanky, he has a pale complexion, and he's wearing a black suit with a stovepipe hat and a tape measure trailing out of his pocket. He has long, skinny fingers that he rubs together in a menacing way whenever he hears of somebody whose health has taken a turn for the worse.

The stereotype of a funeral home is just as rich. Most people see a colonial house where the carpet has a pattern that repeats every six feet. The house smells musty or like old, decaying flowers. It's dark inside, and always in the distance there's the sound of organ music. Just about the time you get comfortable in these surroundings, somebody sneaks up behind you and scares the heck out of you, asking in a slow, low voice, "Can I help you?"

Sound familiar? It should. We've grown up with these stereotypes in movies, television shows, and books. Like all stereotypes, they are exaggerated. For the most part throughout my career, I've had a lot of fun with this because I've never really fit the stereotype of a funeral director. Most funeral directors don't fit this mold, and now that about 50 percent of funeral directors are women, we're gladly moving farther and farther from the stereotype.

The news media hasn't helped with the public's perception of funeral professionals either. When the news covers any story regarding the funeral profession, it's almost always a negative one. They tend to focus on the very few in our profession who are flat-out bad people. These bad apples not only take advantage of the people who are looking to them for help, but they are usually violating state or federal laws. It's hard to get those stories and images from the news out of your head, so you come to the funeral home's doorstep with your guard up from the get-go.

More than ever, you cannot afford to have yourself and your family be influenced by these stereotypes. This is very important because of the widely available information—and misinformation—that is accessible at any time of the day or night via the Internet. These days, anyone with a blog will call himself a journalist, but just because it's published on the web and even if it is widely dispersed, doesn't mean that it came from a reliable, trustworthy, or educated source. The truth is that the web provides much more information than we've ever had access to before, but you have to be very discerning about whether it is true or not.

So, if the information that comes from the Internet has

questionable truthfulness, and you've carried this stereotype of funeral directors and funeral homes for all your life; how do you keep your family from being ripped off when somebody you love dies and you need one of these funeral people?

The good news is most funeral homes in the Midwest (which is the marketplace where I operate) are honest and very good providers of their craft. In fact, for about 12 years of my career, I covered funeral service providers across the entire United States and rarely did I see a funeral home or a funeral director live up to the creepy stereotype.

That said, the shady characters are out there and in order to avoid being ripped off a little bit of discernment on your part is required. Trust your instincts. If the funeral director or home you're working with makes you uncomfortable or makes you feel pressured, you don't have to use them. Also, be critical of price. Sometimes a low price IS too good to be true, and at the end of the memorial you planned, friends and family may feel slighted or further hurt by the unsatisfactory service. If you simply pursue the lowest price, the value you get from the services might not be what you wanted.

There are people who see everyone in our profession as scavengers who swoop in to take advantage of families at a vulnerable time. We do run a business, but we are not out to take advantage of your loss! We're here to provide a service which will help you and your family manage the many arrangements that need to be made at a very difficult time and to ensure that you have a meaningful service that will honor the person who has died and begin to give closure to the survivors. Any funeral home worth dealing with will have these simple goals as their first priority.

QUESTION TWO

WHAT SHOULD I LOOK FOR IN A FUNERAL HOME OR CREMATION PROVIDER?

Let me give you a few ideas on what to look for:

- You definitely want to go to somebody who has a bricks and mortar investment, someone who has a building in your community and has been located there for some time. That's important. That means that they've made a commitment to the community, they operate within the laws, and they are licensed by their state's health department.
- Always look for a good reputation, not just for the funeral home itself, but also for the people working at the funeral home.
- Make sure they have a cooler. This may not be something you'd think of, or want to think about, but it provides an incomparable level of short-term preservation.
- Ask around. Friends and relatives can give invaluable

referrals to good funeral service providers.
- Be sure that you feel comfortable there, not only with the people, but also in the surroundings.
- Make sure that you have contact with a well-educated staff member who can answer questions confidently and put you at ease. You should readily have the feeling that "These people know what they're talking about."
- Ask if they offer access and information across social networks.
- The staff should make you feel like you are supported and that you have an ally.

Always look for a willingness on the part of the funeral home and the funeral director to gain more information and present new and interesting ideas on trends such as cremation, personalization, social media integration, and green funerals. If these interest you, go to a funeral director who can actually have an informed discussion about these trends and present options that allow your family to make the right choices for what you want.

Now more than ever, we find out about illnesses or deaths among our friends and families via the Internet, and more specifically, through social media. You will want to make sure that your funeral home gives you the tools to connect effectively and elegantly with people through social media outlets. Right now, that's one of the most underutilized parts of our profession.

Our website, which I encourage you to visit at www.MuellerMemorial.com, is cutting edge. We allow people to share stories, leave condolences, sign the register book, upload photos and videos, and connect to social networks such as Google Plus, Facebook, and Twitter. Through our connection to the Book of Memories Online Tributes, we are able to maintain a person's memorial page for years to come.

It is also important that your funeral home's website be optimized for mobile devices, as more and more people are relying on their smartphones to access information or get directions. We strive to develop our services to keep pace with technology as it evolves. The funeral home you choose should be doing the same.

The bottom line is that you need to work with someone who will help you to make decisions that are in your family's best interests. I come across many people who know what I do and are a little disgusted by the whole practice of this "American way of death" and the expense of funerals. They will go out of their way to tell me that funerals are overpriced, they don't provide enough value, and that all they'll need to do is simply do the least: get rid of the body and move on. Their thought is "If we get rid of it, we eliminate the pain."

The truth is that the pain of loss doesn't just go away, and many times, because of your response to it now, it can be compounded and become worse and worse over time. A good funeral director's responsibility is to help guide you toward the options that can help you to begin the grief process in the best possible way for you and your family. Your children and your grandchildren learn from your response to death, and if your response is inadequate, then their response may be inadequate throughout their lives.

No matter how much you intellectualize your approach to death, one thing to remember is that you and your family are going to hurt when somebody you love dies. There is no getting away from it. It is something that is going to happen. It is just as certain as the slow recovery after a surgery. You know that to be the case with surgery, and you should know that to be the case with death and grief as well. You are going to hurt.

What you need to ask yourself when choosing a funeral or cremation service provider is "Does the provider care enough to help my family and me adjust to and recover from the death of this person we care so much about?" If the answer is no, then you need to find another service provider.

QUESTION THREE

DOES OWNERSHIP MATTER?

Ownership matters. I mentioned earlier that I had been traveling the country for 12 years. During that time, I had sold my business to a company called Service Corporation International, SCI, based in Houston, Texas. This company owns and operates funeral homes and cemeteries all around the world. I traveled around for them and visited their funeral homes.

I sold my business in 1994, but I just wasn't happy with the direction they were taking the business and the effect it was having on my reputation in the community, so I bought it back in 2005.

It's important for you to realize that now many funeral homes are owned and operated by companies like SCI, or Stewart Enterprises, or one of many regional consolidators. These large, multi-national corporations and regional operators are there for one reason and one reason only: profit.

I was part of it. I sold my business to these people, and I got an inside look at how it happened. Bottom line, their concern is the shareholders. In the year 2011, the president of SCI, Tom Ryan, made several million dollars running a corporation out of Dallas that owns funeral homes and cemeteries all over the country. Their accountability is to shareholders, not to their community, and not to the families they serve. In fact, their business model is not dependent on, nor supportive of, the community in which they operate. All of their profits go back to their headquarters in Texas.

When you hear about poor quality service, or about things that were outright illegal in the profession, many times those incidents come out of the facilities that are owned, at a distance, by large corporations where the funeral home or cremation provider is under remote management.

Local owners, those who own their own funeral home in the community they serve, are involved with and accountable to their neighbors, not their shareholders. Individual owners who have a stake in their community are more interested in keeping their reputation at a much higher level. Look for a funeral home—insist on a funeral home—that is locally owned. It will benefit your family because ownership does matter.

QUESTION FOUR

WHO REGULATES THE FUNERAL PROFESSION?

There is a layer of trust to be found in regulation. Most states regulate funeral homes and each regulates them a little bit differently. Most states require a license for the individual funeral director and one separately for the funeral facility. The state must grant a license to the individual mortician or funeral director before they can practice. Before that license is granted, the funeral director must go through the education process (usually a bachelor's degree in Mortuary Science) that will prepare them to pass the State and National Board exam. A funeral facility and its contents must be inspected and meet very specific standards before a license is awarded. Only Colorado does not require a license.

Funeral homes and funeral directors are usually licensed, but cemetery owners and cemetery operators are not. Cemeteries can be a different situation altogether. There are non-profit and for-profit cemeteries, and sometimes it's very difficult to tell the difference. When looking for a cemetery, it is not critical that you look for a non-profit cemetery, but it is critical to look for one that you really trust and has maintained their grounds well throughout the years. The truth is that the cemetery property will be something that is purchased once but taken care of forever, so you need to know that the property is well maintained and properly funded.

In addition to state regulations, the Federal Trade Commission (FTC) has put into effect a Funeral Trade Rule for funeral homes in all 50 states. Part of this rule says that a general price list will be given to you and a casket, vault, and urn price list will be available to you. You have the right to call and ask for information over the phone. The funeral home is legally obligated to answer any pricing questions you have, be it in person or over the phone. If a funeral home refuses to give you a general price list, they are in violation of the Federal Trade Rule, and you should go elsewhere.

Section Two

Funeral Customs and Traditions

QUESTION FIVE

HOW DID FUNERALS BECOME COMMON?

In the briefest terms, funerals have always been part of human society. Since the time that humans came to be on Earth, there has always been a need to recognize a death. Graves have been found dating back to the Paleolithic era roughly 100,000 years ago. It is actually because of these graves and the items buried with the bodies that we see the first evidence of belief in leaving something with the deceased for the afterlife, and thus the first representation of belief in some sort of transcendence or religion.

The ancient Egyptians were probably the most prominent lovers of funerals, because of the now famous elaborate graves that they made in the form of pyramids. These pyramids, where the Pharaohs were buried, were very intricate mazes of passages and chambers which housed riches, and sometimes even servants that accompanied the Pharaoh's carefully tended body to the underworld so that he would be able to enjoy the same wealth he had experienced in his life on Earth. Caring for the dead, celebrating their life, and marking their passage to the afterlife are traditions that have been around for millennia. Actually, the Greek word for funeral, κηδεία, means to tend to or take care of someone.

Cremation is also a very long-standing death ritual with evidence of it dating back 20,000 years. The early Romans famously used cremation as a form of military honor. The Vikings would also honor their dead by building thoughtfully constructed pyres, which would burn with great intensity and create towering columns of smoke to usher the deceased into the afterlife.

Throughout civilization, these ceremonies gave the survivors an opportunity to honor the deceased, and allowed them to participate in one final act of caring for their friend or family member. This desire to come together, to be involved in creating support and acknowledgement for the loss of life, is something that we as humans feel compelled to do to this day.

Society has always recognized a need for coming together when a death happens. But, I fear that Facebook is replacing the inherent obligation for people to come together at a funeral. When a notification of a death is made via Facebook (which can be a very efficient way to get the information out to people) some will just comment "You are in my thoughts and prayers." It's a very kind sentiment and it may be appropriate for an acquaintance, but being in their thoughts and prayers will never replace being face-to-face with a person who has just experienced the death of a family member or friend. We are social beings, and as such, we have a need to share tears, feel a hug, and hear empathy in voices. Nothing will ever replace the comfort of gathering after a death.

QUESTION SIX

HOW DID THE PRACTICE OF EMBALMING BEGIN?

We have to go back to the Civil War to find the origins of embalming in America. Back then, there were many boys killed so far away from home, and the desire to bring the body back to the family fostered the practice of embalming.

Embalming was a way to replace the blood with, at that time, a compound of arsenic. Arsenic is an extraordinarily good preservative. Unfortunately, it's also an extraordinarily good poison. So, the use of arsenic was predominately replaced with formaldehyde.

Embalming was performed during the Civil War to serve two purposes. First, it preserved the body for the lengthy journey back to the soldier's home where services and burial would take place. Second, it preserved the body in such a manner that it allowed the family a decent presentation so that they could have their chance to say goodbye.

Embalming allowed funerals to take place sometime after the death and to be a more pleasant experience than they had been in the past. Prior to embalming, the closest thing we had to preserving the body during the funeral ceremonies and services was to place the body on blocks of ice. Many times, this was done in the parlor of the family home.

QUESTION SEVEN

HOW DID FUNERAL DIRECTION BECOME A PROFESSION?

In the past, many homes were built with both a parlor and a living room. And the parlor's purpose was for ceremonial events and funerals.

Funerals were held in the home, the visitation was held in the home, and even after embalming became common, the funeral director would go out to the home and embalm the body in the kitchen. This was usually done by taking a door down and using that as the preparation table. As that got more cumbersome for more people, it was determined that there ought to be a professional who does this in the community.

At the time, mostly cabinet and furniture makers were in charge of funerals because a furniture company had a facility that was big enough to be rearranged so that a funeral could be performed there. In addition, the furniture makers had the ability to make suitable burial containers, which began the tradition of beautifully crafted wooden caskets. It's not unusual to go into a small town today and see a furniture company and the funeral home owned by the same family.

Less and less, families wanted to hold funerals in their home, or even had a home big enough to do it. More and more, people wanted services to be performed in a funeral home or a funeral parlor. Thus, funeral parlors and funeral directors came to be.

QUESTION EIGHT

DO I NEED A CHURCH?

In the past, funerals always revolved around aspects of religion and clergy, so there was always a strong connection to the church. Churches have been an important place for funeral services throughout history. That's becoming less common, as organized religion is becoming less significant to many people today. It's a bit of a harsh reality, but it's true. I am struck by the number of people now who tell me "Dad was very spiritual, but he wasn't religious."

Recently, a man's daughter came in just two minutes before the funeral service started, and said to the priest "Father, my dad was a devout Catholic, but he didn't go to church." Generally, in the Catholic faith being considered "devout" and regularly attending church are inextricably linked. In this case, the priest understood that though the deceased wasn't necessarily active in the church, it was very important to his survivors that he receive the rites consistent with his faith.

With fewer and fewer people associated with a church, funeral services are increasingly taking place at the funeral home, somebody's country club, a house, or a ballroom. Some are elaborate catered events at event centers with live music. Really, the options for location are limited only by budget, geography, and your imagination.

Often now, rather than using a member of the clergy to administer the services, the events are being presided over by a funeral celebrant. A funeral celebrant is somebody who is usually not ordained, but is trained to present a very personal type of funeral service specific to the desires of the deceased or their family without the restrictions often imposed by organized religious ceremonies. At these types of ceremonies, you can customize the atmosphere, play popular music, and do just about anything you want to celebrate a life.

I don't want to minimize the connection between death and the Church. Many people feel closer to their own spirituality at the time of a friend or family member's death, or at the time just before their own death. There is certainly comfort and hope to be found in the scriptures and traditions of the Church, and many see those as indispensable parts of the grieving process. Many religions have very specific rituals that must be performed at the time of death in order to usher the soul safely into the afterlife. If the deceased was a very religious person in their life, they will likely want to adhere to the rites of their religion at the time of their death.

QUESTION NINE

HOW CAN I PERSONALIZE A FUNERAL?

Funerals have always allowed for a great deal of personalization. However, the G.I. Generation, those who grew up during the Great Depression and World War II, the generation of many of our parents who are now in their eighties and nineties, they really trusted the funeral director to pretty much make the plans for them because most of them followed the same traditions and customs.

But now, as Baby Boomers get older and want to express their own unique personalities, they're getting much more personal with how they want to be remembered. They want one last chance to be able to say, "Hey, I mattered. I was one of a kind, and this is how I want to be remembered!" So, for the Boomers, lots of personalization takes place and it's expanding all the time.

As an example, one of the people we served was an avid golfer, so in the obituary it was noted that all of the attendees were requested to wear golf attire. As people began to arrive, there was a colorful crowd of argyle socks, bright sweater vests over collared shirts, knickerbockers, and newsboy caps. It instantly created a festive atmosphere and brought a degree of levity to the service, which was the full intention of the golfer being celebrated.

Another example was, sadly, a younger woman who had died and was very fond of having her fingernails painted. In the middle of our Great Room, we set up a table for people to have their nails painted in her favorite color.

We have also served an artist, and when it was time for his services we took all of our art down off the walls and replaced it with his original works, turning it into something more like a gallery show.

These people knew and expressed what they wanted, or they had someone acting on their behalf that was creative enough to think outside of the traditions and to give a more unique meaning to their memorial.

These are the types of people from whom you hear about the possibilities of ashes being shot into space, made into a wreath, or have the carbon siphoned off to make a diamond. Those types of options are becoming very, very significant to a population that increasingly wants something that is different from the other guy, and the people helping to arrange the funeral can help make those things possible.

The person you choose as a funeral director should be able to help personalize the service and offer suggestions on how you can further customize this event for you and your family. If they can't, you should move on. And if their extent of personalization is just putting a picture on a card, that isn't enough anymore.

At Mueller Memorial, we've been doing custom video montages since 1988, and we continue to refine the quality and production value to make that video something meaningful you can come back to for years. But videos are just the beginning; the options are truly endless! The key is planning. No one likes to think about the reality of his or her own funeral, but if you do, you put yourself in a position to make your wishes known and in no uncertain terms.

So many people say, "At my funeral, I don't want a bunch of people standing around being sad." Well, in order to remove the risk that someone will plan that type of funeral for you, you need to make your wishes known. Write them down. Let people know.

Of course, you'll write down the things that you like, but just as important are your dislikes. If you can't stand gladiolas, write that down. If you've never cared for On Eagles Wings, make sure someone knows that. If you take the time to think about the details of your funeral, then you'll get the type of celebration that you want. We'll get more into the additional benefits of complete pre-planning a little bit later.

Section Three

The Function of Funerals

QUESTION TEN

WHY HAVE A FUNERAL?

The simple answer is, someone died and we have to take care of the body. But we all know that funerals and the emotions that surround death are much more complicated than that.

Recently, I was struck by a conversation I had with a friend at a party. The man is an attorney and he's well educated. He had recently buried his mom and proceeded to go on and on telling me about what he doesn't like about the funeral business: that people don't get value for the money spent, and that he doesn't understand why all the pomp and circumstance is needed. He wasn't expressing sadness or loss, just negativity toward the funeral profession. His position was that all anyone needed to do was just get rid of the body and be done with it, but I know from years of experience that it's just not that simple.

This friend's dog had died about three months prior, so we talked about his dog, and within five minutes, he has big tears that are welling up in his eyes as he's talking lovingly about his dog that he had to put down, and how hard it was, and how much he missed that dog. It was an unabashed display of emotion and grief.

At that moment, I looked at him and said, "Bob, why do you

show more emotion for your pet than your parent?"

He said, "What do you mean?"

I said, "You've talked more about what you felt for your pet, than what you felt for your parent when she died."

We live in cynical times and it's difficult for people who are afraid of displaying their emotions to grieve openly, because they have some notion that they need to keep a stiff upper lip or be strong. Funeral services are an emotional safe zone. People expect emotion at these services and it gives even the stiffest upper lip permission to tremble a bit.

The truth is that very few people have been taught how to really deal with loss of any kind. It simply doesn't exist in our society. So when loss happens, we feel it is unfair, that we don't deserve it, and that we shouldn't have to experience it.

A funeral is the best way to confront the death of a family member or a friend, and be surrounded at that time by sympathetic and supportive familiars.

Recently, with the growth of cremation, many funerals are delayed because the body has been cremated already and the ashes exist in their final state, so there's no urgency to have the funeral. Often a family will elect to wait until a funeral is more convenient for them. So, they put it together with a birthday or their Thanksgiving celebration or a wedding, or some other family event. I'm not convinced that this is the best way to go about it. I'm amazed that we even think about the possibility of funerals being convenient. Death is anything but convenient. When a death takes place, we should stop our lives, if only for a moment. It's reasonable to stop everything for a couple of days and just pay attention to the people who most need our help: the family who is grieving this loss.

If we wait for a funeral to become convenient, it will be overpowered by (or put a damper on) the fun of the wedding or the holiday celebration. We celebrate Thanksgiving every year. We celebrate Christmas every year. Yet many people insist that coming together for the death of somebody we love is less important. They simply cremate them and move on with their life. Then weeks later, they wonder why they can't be productive, why they can't get anything done, or why they suddenly have an urge to cry at the strangest times. What happens to the immediate family in the time between the death and the event or holiday? They are still going through grief, but without the personal support one gets at a funeral. They also have this unfinished business of the weeks-away memorial service weighing on their minds. There is no greater time to come together and to help the family than at the time of the death.

I think the reason most people don't want to get together at that time is that it's uncomfortable. Many people don't know what to say, and the truth is that you don't have to know what to say. All you have to do is be present. Sometimes all you need to do is open up your arms, hug that person, and just say these simple words: I'm so sorry. That is all that anyone can expect of you.

Funerals these days can take on many different forms. They can have the body present or not. They can have the ashes present or not. They can be in a church or not. In its simplest forms, the common threads of every funeral are:
- Somebody we love or care for has died.
- The body must be taken care of.

The body must be cremated or buried. Right now, it's about 50 percent either cremation or burial. Beyond those two very basic elements, we can be very creative with how a funeral service can be done, so that during the process of that funeral, we can have some of the major emotions come out: laughter, tears, sorrow, regret, delight, and fun. A well-positioned, well-done funeral can have a significant emotional impact on those attending, and can help lay the foundation for their grieving process. This is why we have a funeral.

QUESTION ELEVEN

CAN WE PULL OFF THIS EVENT IN THREE DAYS?

One thing that parents have in common is that they are probably going to go through planning a wedding. A wedding today averages about $27,000, and it's a great event that involves months, if not years, of preparation. The amazing thing is that, with our divorce rate, 50 percent of people who have had a wedding are destined to repeat that situation again, thus paying another $27,000 for another "once-in-a-lifetime" event.

A funeral can cost one-fourth to one-third of that. We plan, organize, and carry out all the services and events, in a highly personalized way, usually within three or four days of the death. Some people who have a year to plan their wedding hire a wedding planner because there is so much to keep track of. When planning a funeral, an event of similar magnitude, in such a short period, it absolutely makes sense to have someone there to help inform your decisions. Someone to hire a bagpiper, book a hall, arrange catering, process official documentation for death certificates, make a balloon arch, find a guy who does dove releases, bring in some sandwiches, let the Reverend know it's spelled Hamor but it's pronounced Hay-mer, set up easels for your photo boards, secure permits for burial or cremation, make sure that the bagpiper and the dove guy get paid, haul flowers, and find you some time alone time when you need it. Someone to take care of all the things you don't want to worry about on a day when all you want to do is consider your lost friend or family member. And all of this for what is guaranteed to be a once-in-a-lifetime event.

So, the answer is yes, funeral directors can pull all of this off and more in three or four days. They have the contacts and the know-how to get things done quickly the way you want, while relieving you of much of the burden of organizing.

QUESTION TWELVE

WHAT IS THE VALUE OF A VIEWING?

Traditionally with burials, the body is viewed as part of the service. This is commonly called a visitation.

With cremation, there may not be a standard or a traditional visitation, and that's okay. But, what must happen for every family's sake is to be given the opportunity to say goodbye to that body, and to view that body prior to the cremation or to the burial.

Once cremation starts, it can't be stopped. We need to allow the family time to say goodbye to that person, even though that lifeless person is not the soul that we knew just hours before.

I'm always struck by the family who says, "We cared for him up until his death. Why would you want us to view him again? Why would we need to do that?"

And my answer's always the same: "What you did for him up till the time that he died was all about his final struggle—his final breaths, his final moments on this earth—it was all about caring for that live body. But now things have changed. They've drastically changed, and in order for you to move on, it is best for you to have time with that person now in their current state and to realize that this change has taken place."

You'd be surprised how many people can't embrace the reality of the death if they are not able to see the body. It's one of the things that funeral directors most strongly encourage people to do—and it's one of the things that people dread the most.

If you're opting for direct cremation, you do not have to have embalming, nor have the body cosmetized (made up), nor have the body specially dressed at all, but you do have to have a moment before the burial or cremation that allows you to say goodbye to that which we identify with the soul: the unique mortal body.

For the same reasons that I encourage families to view the body, I also encourage them to host a public visitation. For a public visitation at our funeral home, we do require embalming and cosmetizing, but these extra steps afford people outside the immediate family the opportunity to also say their final goodbyes and confront the reality of the death of their friend or extended family member.

You may not know it, but a death impacts people who may be rather far removed from your or the deceased person's life. Allowing extended family and friends to see the body allows them to make peace with the fact that this person is no longer alive. It sounds over simplistic, but it's possible that the last time that person saw the deceased, he or she was healthy and vibrant. So, it's helpful for this extension of your family and friends to be offered the chance to come to grips with the death as well.

If you're having more traditional services, a visitation is usually done by way of an evening Open House, which also caters to the needs of extended family and friends. The Open House format means that people who may be on the periphery of your life, but still want the opportunity to say their goodbyes and offer their support to the family, have the chance to do that without having to take off a day of work or attend a lengthy service.

If someone is adamant against being viewed after they've died, you can still hold something similar to a visitation in the form of a reception. Or, if you're feeling adventurous, you could offer beer and wine like a Happy Hour, or, as one of our more witty clients called it, "an Unhappy Hour."

Section Four

Burial Services

QUESTION THIRTEEN

WHAT'S INVOLVED IN FULL BURIAL SERVICES?

For generations, the common approach toward a funeral was to have the body carried to a cemetery and buried in the ground. This has been the way that we have done things for many, many years. When I first started in this profession in the Seventies, only about three percent of people were cremated, 97 percent were buried in the earth.

Usually, but not always, other items and services go into full burial. Generally, there are a casket, a vault, a cemetery plot, services to open and close the ground, then a marker for the plot. Once someone is buried, that plot of land is designated as a cemetery, and as such, can never be used for any other purpose—ever.

Everybody has a cemetery near his or her home. Cemeteries are an interesting place to walk. I suggest taking a stroll through a cemetery sometime. It's not as uncomfortable as some might think. You'll find that you can get a real sense of the history of the community by looking at the markers that cover the grounds. And those markers will be there for a long time to come.

A cemetery plot is a unique purchase. A grave is purchased with a one-time payment. After that, there are no property taxes or maintenance costs. The cemetery will be maintained and that grave will be maintained for eternity. The grass will be cut, the curbs will be trimmed, and the trees will be groomed forever. A cemetery plot can be, overall, one of the most inexpensive parts of a funeral when you look at it from a long-term value perspective.

With the current trend of "going green," some people have expressed opposition to taking up space when someone is buried. Burial plots are not a detriment to the environment. When you realize that what I said in the previous paragraph is true, and that the plot you purchase has legally got to be maintained ad infinitum, what you end up doing is sustaining a 24 square foot area of urban, suburban, or rural green space. If you think of it that way, it's quite the ecological memorial. If you live in the Twin Cities area, all you need to do is visit Lakewood Cemetery in Minneapolis to see how really peaceful and beautiful a memorial garden in an urban setting can be.

QUESTION FOURTEEN

IS A CASKET REQUIRED?

Most states do not require that a casket be used for burial. I know that sounds strange, because most think that a casket is necessary for burial.

A casket is the most traditional and efficient way to present and transport a body throughout the services. A casket in Roman times was a box designed to carry something precious—and it does. But more than that, a casket is designed to enhance the viewing of the body. The choice of a casket is one of the more traditional opportunities one has to personalize a part of the funeral services. There are many options ranging from elegant wood creations to sports-themed caskets to the emblems of religion to the strength of metals.

QUESTION FIFTEEN

CAN I GET A CASKET ELSEWHERE?

Yes, caskets are available from Costco, the Internet, your funeral home, and in some marketplaces, even a store whose sole purpose is to sell caskets. You do not have to buy a casket from a funeral home. What's more, a funeral home cannot charge a markup (a handling fee or a service fee) to you for purchasing a casket elsewhere.

You can also construct your own casket, as long as it is strong enough and will not diminish the integrity of the body inside or threaten the health and safety of the employees of funeral home who must take care of it.

Any quick Google search of caskets will give you all sorts of sources to buy caskets. Be aware that those casket prices may look inexpensive, and many of them include free shipping, which seems like a great deal, but the free shipping is usually within seven to 10 days. And it must be shipped to a funeral home. Most funeral homes need the casket sooner than that, so in addition to the casket price, you're going to pay a quick ship fee, which can be $500 or more. Ordering a casket like that could come with hidden fees that really hike the price up.

More and more, funeral homes are pricing their caskets competitively with the total cost of caskets found on the internet. If you come to my funeral home, the casket prices here are as good as, or better than, what you will see across the web. I'm able to buy from a vendor where I negotiate discount terms and I pass that savings over to the family. It allows me to provide a better deal.

I can also get delivery directly from the manufacturer, rather than a casket store or an internet provider. Outside casket sources may need to have the casket sent to an affiliate funeral home to crate it up, ship it to the nearest airport, and then have a common carrier pick it up and deliver it. Throughout this time, you have to make sure that the product isn't damaged, and many times that's difficult to promise. All those steps make for a lot more unnecessary concern for the family, when the funeral home can get direct delivery at a very comparable price.

Can buying a casket on the internet save you money? Possibly, but many times, a funeral home can find something at a similar quality and price. Simply bring the complete quoted price in to the funeral home and say, "Listen, I saw this online. Have you got something comparable to it?"

QUESTION SIXTEEN

WHY DOES THE STATE REQUIRE A VAULT?

States don't require a vault. It's commonly thought that they do because an outside liner is usually required for almost every cemetery.

So why is it necessary? Well, the cemetery sets rules on this, and the reason why they want an outside burial enclosure, or a burial vault, to be used is because, regardless of the casket that you select, it will never be strong enough to withhold the weight of the earth above it over time. In fact, in old sections of a cemetery you'll see the headstones will be a little askew and the ground will be uneven, that is because over time the caskets have collapsed under the ground.

Cemeteries require an outside burial container simply because it makes the grounds easier to maintain. These outside enclosures are made of steel or concrete, and because they are reinforced, they are strong enough to withstand not only the weight of the earth above it, but the dynamic load that comes from running tractors and heavy equipment over it. More importantly, it assures that the grave beneath will not be disturbed when an adjacent grave is being dug. The equipment that's being used at cemeteries today is stronger and more powerful than ever, so vaults maintain the integrity of the surrounding graves.

A definition of "burial container" should be made here. The cemetery requires an outside burial container, and I'm using the word vault, but technically, they are not the same. An outside burial container is a broad term that includes vaults, but it also includes a non-sealed concrete box, or a box that may be constructed without a bottom portion, but the sides and the top are in place to provide the necessary support.

People who want the container sealed select a burial vault. Usually, depending on selection, vaults are sealed against the entrance of air and water, two of the most corrosive substances that can affect the condition of the casket and the body. Is it important that these things be sealed? It is only important if it's important to you. The truth is that the cemetery doesn't require it be sealed or not, they just require that some kind of burial container be used. So, a burial vault is a matter of personal preference.

QUESTION SEVENTEEN

WHY IS EMBALMING REQUIRED?

Many times, embalming is not required. Now, this takes a little bit of frank explanation, and I am speaking strictly about my state, which is Minnesota. The rules vary from state to state, but Minnesota allows 72 hours between the time of death and the time of burial or cremation (both known as a means of final disposition) before the body is recognized as becoming a health hazard and then embalming is required.

Seventy-two hours is three days, and that's usually enough time to arrange for either a cremation or a burial service if you do not want to embalm. However, if you want to have a visitation where the public may be invited, then the funeral director may require embalming. And there's a good reason for that.

When someone dies, decomposition begins immediately. It begins in a variety of different ways, but suffice to say that within three days, there can be a lot of changes to a body. That body can also be affected by the weather conditions, such as humidity. So, after three days, it may not be safe or pleasant for the public to be around a body that has not been embalmed.

I'm licensed by the Department of Public Health to protect the public health, which includes my employees, and all the people who walk in my door as well. As such, I take that 72-hour limit very seriously. I never embalm as a means to add on a fee; I do it simply as a means to protect the public's health, or at the request of the family.

Many people wonder why a cooler is not used. Most funeral homes don't have a cooler simply because, historically, they haven't needed them. When I was first licensed, nearly all bodies were embalmed. Embalming is a very effective way to preserve a body, so a cooler wasn't needed. With cremation becoming more popular now, there is less embalming so the use of a cooler like ours allows for better natural temporary preservation.

QUESTION EIGHTEEN

WHAT ARE THE OPTIONS AND COSTS OF FULL BURIAL?

Burial options and costs will likely involve several different things, including:
- Funeral home services and facilities
- Transportation
- The casket
- The vault
- The cemetery plot
- The opening and closing of the plot
- A marker for the gravesite
- Additional costs from musicians, clergy, and so on

Depending on the cemetery that you select, there will be a price for the grave, and then, at the time that you need to use that grave, there will be a price for the opening and closing of that grave (the digging of that grave).

Additionally, if you want to mark the grave, there will be a marker expense. Some cemeteries may require a flat marker only. If you want to have an upright marker, the cemetery usually requires the purchase of four or more graves. Cemeteries restrict the option for upright markers not to make it more expensive for you to buy, but to make it less expensive for them to maintain. Upright markers are more difficult to mow around and to care for over time. Every cemetery has its own rules about markers. They also have their own price structures, and these can depend on any number of variables.

It's important to note that although we're talking about the burial of a body, ashes can be buried as well. Most cemeteries have several different options for the burial of ashes. Some cemeteries have beautiful, above ground buildings or small niche banks that are usually above ground, which elegantly house the ashes. These are commonly called a columbarium or mausoleum.

Some cemeteries have ossuaries or cremation gardens, which are creative options for the burial of ashes. These in-ground burial areas are exclusively intended for ashes, so the plots are smaller and often less costly. As you can see, there are quite a few things to think about when deciding amongst burial options.

If your family already owns a gravesite, and there are family members already buried in the cemetery, most cemeteries will allow you to access a grave with an existing burial in it and only pay a right of second interment to bury the ashes of another individual in that same grave. This way, you do not have to pay the full purchase price of another gravesite. You simply pay a fee for the right of that second interment (or burial), which allows you to put another marker on that grave. In addition to the fee for the right of second interment, there will also be an opening and closing fee. There is usually a limit of two interments per plot and at least one of them has to be burial of cremated ashes.

Section Five

Cremation Services

QUESTION NINETEEN

DO FUNERAL HOMES OFFER CREMATION?

Funeral homes provide cremation and always have. The problem is that it's never really advertised because, as recently as the Seventies, better than 95 percent of the funerals that took place were burial and not cremation-related.

Cremation is something that has been around for millennia. The Catholic Church really took a dim view of cremation because it was seen as a pagan ritual or as an act of outright defiance toward the Catholic idea of resurrection. The Catholic Church has reconciled their feeling towards cremation and now allows cremation to take place.

Funeral homes offer cremation, but very few funeral homes actually own their own crematory. Most funeral homes will have an arrangement with a local crematory. It is important to ask the funeral home: "What crematory do you use?" and "What security measures do they have in place to protect the deceased?" A little later, I'll go in-depth on why these questions are so important.

You may wonder why funeral homes don't have their own crematory. Well, a crematory is an industrial piece of equipment with a slight potential for discharge into the atmosphere. So, from that standpoint, crematories are more difficult to construct in residential neighborhoods, where most funeral homes are. Most crematories are located in an industrial area or in the middle of a cemetery.

QUESTION TWENTY

WHAT'S THE DIFFERENCE BETWEEN A FUNERAL HOME AND A CREMATION SOCIETY?

Most major marketplaces have, in addition to funeral homes, a cremation society. Cremation societies give the appearance of being a non-profit organization and that they help provide the least expensive service. Usually, this is not the case.

Cremation societies are often funeral homes presenting themselves as some kind of association or organization.

In my state of Minnesota, the largest cremation society is a funeral home, just with a different name. They focus almost exclusively on cremation, and usually lead with a very enticing price.

Most of these are very low priced because of the volume of cremation that they do. This is because they're able to keep their crematories operating almost 24 hours a day and they are engineered to provide a very limited range of services for people.

As we discussed earlier, funeral services are the chance to come together to honor the person who has died. The funeral will lay the foundation for the survivors' grieving process, so this may not be the time to sacrifice service for a lower price.

When I am asked "What's the difference between a cremation society and a funeral home?" I always tell people that if you want a cremation society to handle the cremation of somebody that you love, just ask them what assurance they can give you that the ashes that you get back are the ones of the person you love. Wait for the blank stare and the long silence that you will likely get.

The truth is that many are like a machine for processing bodies into ashes, which do not have a mechanism to assure you that the ashes that you get back are in fact the ones of the person that you love.

A funeral home should be asked the same questions about ensuring the ashes you receive are those of your friend or family member, and their response should be the kind of response that increases your level of trust and decreases your level of anxiety. If they are not able to answer this to your satisfaction, whether they are a funeral home or cremation society, you should walk out the door and choose another provider. Find a provider where you feel you can be assured that your family would be well taken care of with integrity, honesty, and careful consideration.

QUESTION TWENTY-ONE

WITH CREMATION, IS A CASKET REQUIRED?

A casket is never required for cremation. You may choose one if you like, but a casket is not required. Most states require that the body be placed in at least a minimum alternative container, or canvas bag. The minimum alternative container is defined a little differently from state to state, but usually it is something that is rigid, leak-proof, completely covers the body, and has some signage on it identifying it as mortal remains and who the person inside is.

In our profession, rental caskets are one of the most widely accepted things that are not advertised. We call it a ceremonial casket, but most everybody knows it as a rental. It has a one-time use alternative container interior (required for transport and cremation) that has been designed to fit into a reusable solid exterior casket. This way the outside casket is reused, but the interior that houses the alternative container and the interior upholstery of the casket are removable. The body comes out in the alternative container; there's a top put on it, and then the casket is relined with a new alternative container, with new upholstery. That is to say, that every part of the casket the body is in contact with goes with the body into cremation. Only the outermost part is reused.

Ceremonial caskets can be an inexpensive way to be able to have a traditional visitation and church service, but not have to make the financial commitment of buying a casket for someone who will be cremated.

QUESTION TWENTY-TWO

WHAT HAPPENS DURING CREMATION?

A crematory is, essentially, a large brick oven. A crematory has two chambers in it: the main chamber where the body is placed and the afterburner. The afterburner is usually below the main chamber and refractory brick surrounds both chambers.

Before the body is put into the crematory, the afterburner is started. The afterburner is started first because the crematory has to get to a certain temperature. If it doesn't, then the burning of the container will create smoke and a great deal of concern in the community. Once the chamber gets to about 1,000 degrees, the body is placed into the main chamber. The main chamber will fire then, and the crematory will operate at a temperature of 1,600 to 1,900 degrees. It will burn for about an hour and a half to two hours, and then there's a cool down time.

Modern day cremators are able to function without any disturbance to the surrounding community by not creating a noticeable smell, sound, or smoke. You could be standing right outside of one and never even know it is working.

What's left after cremation are really not ashes at all, but simply the elements of the bone that cannot be consumed by fire. These remains are meticulously removed by the operator and then put into a processor that will pulverize the bones to an indistinguishable, granular size. These are commonly referred to as ashes, but really, they are elements of bone.

If the body was in a casket, or a cardboard container, those containers will have been totally consumed. There will be no ash left from any wood or any cardboard. If there were any metal implants in the body, they would survive the cremation, but be separated out. Titanium can be recycled.

If you choose cremation, you also have the right to be able to go to the crematory when the cremation takes place. A few families prefer to do this as a way to give them peace of mind and to be absolutely assured that everything was done correctly.

QUESTION TWENTY-THREE

HOW DO I KNOW THAT THE ASHES I GET ARE THOSE OF THE ONE I LOVE?

When I sit down with a family that chooses cremation, I know they'll have two questions on their mind, so I bring them up right away. And when I do, their heads start to nod.

The first question is "How do I know that the ashes I get back are of the person I love?" And the second question is "How do I know that you didn't cremate more than one person at time?"

When I discuss this with a family, here are the assurances I give:

- We want you and your family to come in to identify the body in the container that you selected. The state does require that the body be placed into at least a minimum container, and in our case, the minimum container that we have is of the quality that would not embarrass us and would not embarrass the family[1] , and they're going to see it. So the identification of the body takes place.

- During the identification process, we have them sign a very detailed cremation authorization, which explains the process of cremation and exactly what will happen from a procedural standpoint.
- At the time they sign the authorization, they identify a stainless steel bracelet that has a unique number on it. The family watches as this irremovable bracelet is put around the decedent's wrist and the number on the bracelet is noted.
- When the ashes are returned, they come back with this bracelet, and the numbers are still visible. We check to make sure that the numbers on the bracelet are consistent with those on the authorization form.
- When the ashes are processed, all of these things are checked again.

Through this process, the family can be assured that the ashes are those of the one they love. Most high-volume cremators cannot provide that level of assurance, and it is worth asking about.

---

[1] Some funeral homes use minimum containers that are so inexpensive that even *they* are ashamed, and prefer not to let the family see it.

QUESTION TWENTY-FOUR

WHAT CAN I USE FOR AN URN?

The answer to this question, also addresses several other questions. You do not have to buy an urn from the funeral home. Urns can be procured in many different ways. It can be purchased as an urn or it might be a jar, or maybe a personal item. Many of our families have given us things of a personal nature to use as an urn. Here are just a few of the items that we've used as urns:

- ski boots
- hunting muff
- minnow bucket
- sewing cabinet
- tool chest
- cookie jar

Some of these may sound a little strange, but the truth is that they meant something significant to the family. I'll admit that I thought the minnow bucket was a little weird, but when the family and friends came in, they knew it was because he loved to fish, and he'd had that darn thing since he was a kid, and so it's absolutely appropriate.

So as long as it is secure enough and there is enough volume to hold all of the ashes, we can use just about anything for an urn. You do not have to buy it from a funeral home. That said, the range of urns that are available is amazing. Usually funeral homes have a representative sampling of what might be available, and they can range from very traditional to cutting edge.

Following the trend toward "going green", there are biodegradable urns. These urns are made of paper that will degrade so that you can easily float the ashes into a lake or a river and within minutes it will gently sink to the bottom and the paper will disintegrate so that there's no impact to the environment.

We offer a biodegradable urn that's cored from a solid piece of rock salt that can be either buried or put into the water. Within days, the salt will dissolve and the ashes will naturally disperse.

We have bronze sculptures that are beautiful pieces of artwork that can be displayed in your home. No one, except you, needs to know what it really is.

Cremation jewelry has been around for some time, but now it's taken a completely different tack. Most of the jewelry is designed to be filled with a small sample of ashes, which are secured within and can then be worn around the neck. We offer a set of cufflinks that have ashes in them, as well as bracelets, dog tags, and many other types of jewelry. In addition to that, we have jewelry charms made from a fingerprint of the person who has died that are quite beautiful and are elegant, subtle conversation pieces.

One of the most unusual services that we offer is Life Gem. Life Gem will take a sampling of the ashes, siphon the carbon off them, and make a diamond that is uniquely fabricated from this person's ashes. You can choose the size of the diamond, and even to some extent, the color of them. This option can be expensive and can take months to perform, but the results are uniquely beautiful.

QUESTION TWENTY-FIVE

WHAT CAN I DO WITH THE ASHES?

The state looks at the process of cremation as a final disposition of the body, and as such, the remains of the body are no longer a public health concern for the state. This means that you can do almost anything with the ashes. You can scatter them in your yard if you wish. You can scatter them elsewhere.

There are very few limitations on what you can't do, but some examples are that you cannot go onto private property where you don't have permission, and you can't scatter ashes at a national park or a cemetery.

The idea of scattering ashes has been romanticized in the movies and in writing, and it's anything but. The process of scattering ashes can really be quite messy, and that's why we have options such as a rock salt or paper urn. The ashes can be released into water without problems in dispersal.

Ashes can be divided and portions of them given to members of the family, or buried, or scattered in different areas if you wish. Ashes can be held until the time of the death of another family member so that their ashes can be buried together. It's worth noting that if the second person to die is not cremated, the held ashes could be buried in the other person's casket without any additional fees, because there is only one opening and closing of a grave and one plot.

Ashes are easily shipped. However, the only carrier service that will ship cremated remains is the United States Postal Service. UPS and FedEx will not allow ashes to be shipped.

Many times, when a cremation takes place elsewhere, and the ashes are to be brought back home for a service, the family may wish to carry those onto the airplane, and they can. They just have to be in a container that would be TSA compliant, so that when they go through the x-ray machine, there are no questions as to what it might be. You also need to carry with you the Certificate of Cremation that was given to you by the funeral director or cremation service.

QUESTION TWENTY-SIX

DOES THE CATHOLIC CHURCH ALLOW CREMATION?

The Catholic Church has always allowed for cremation, but it's certainly much easier now than it used to be. When I first entered the profession, we used to have to call the archdiocese to get permission for cremation, and permission had to be granted by the archbishop. Cremation had to be done out of personal desire, and not to deny the resurrection of the body.

The only requirement that still exists for Catholics is that the ashes be buried in their entirety in a cemetery. It does not have to be a Catholic cemetery, but the ashes must be buried in a cemetery, and they are not to be divided up. One-hundred percent of the ashes are to be buried.

The Catholic Church strongly prefers that the body be brought into the church for the funeral service, as they have always had a strong reverence for the body. It is not a requirement, however, so cremation could take place first and the ashes brought into church for Mass.

QUESTION TWENTY-SEVEN

WHAT IS GREEN CREMATION?

Green cremation is a name for a process called alkaline hydrolysis. Green cremation is quite a misnomer. The truth is there's really nothing especially "green" about alkaline hydrolysis.

Instead of the body being reduced to bone fragments by flame, it is reduced to bone by pressure, steam, and the use of a very alkali chemical. In two to four hours, under the right conditions, all of the protein, amino acids, skin, flesh, organs are all reduced to slurry. The slurry is then released into the waste system as inert liquid. What's left behind is the skeleton, which is dried and then pulverized to resemble ashes.

There is about 30 percent more volume in ash after a body has been hydrolyzed when compared to a typical cremation. Most people, quite honestly, do not easily accept this process.

When alkaline hydrolysis is explained to most people, they tend to cringe and want to recoil from it. The reason why some funerals homes are embracing it is because it does not have any smoke and therefore it's easier to get that equipment approved for use in their community.

However, the effect of putting that much effluence into the wastewater has been poorly studied, and the jury is still out. Green cremation is a marketing term, and is meant to re-position cremation as environmentally friendly.

Section Six

The Issue of Cost

QUESTION TWENTY-EIGHT

HOW MUCH IS A FUNERAL?

That's a question I am asked quite often, and I can answer it only after I've been able to ask these questions:

- Do you prefer burial or cremation?
- Will you be involving a church or not?
- Do you wish to have the body prepared for a visitation?
- What optional amenities do you want?

The answers to those questions give me an idea of what the charges are going to be. Funeral costs always fall into one of two different categories:

- Funeral service charges, which include the fees associated with the items and services provided by the funeral home such as use of the facilities, automotive equipment, and the merchandise that you select (the merchandise can be a casket, a burial vault, flowers, stationary items, the urn).
- Cash advances are those things associated with a funeral, but they're not provided directly by the funeral home, such as the newspaper obituary notice, the death certificate cost, the church stipend, the organist, the soloist, and the fee for opening and closing the grave. These are related to the

funeral and are managed by the funeral home, but the charges are incurred outside of the funeral home.

The funeral home usually will handle the distribution of payments for you, and then collect the grand total amount from you once all the planning is complete.

To give you an estimate of the costs, cash advances for burial service can range anywhere from $1,000 to $2,500. Expenses for a burial service with a visitation can range anywhere from, $6,000 to over $12,000. Most funerals cost less than $10,000.

QUESTION TWENTY-NINE

HOW MUCH DOES CREMATION COST?

Some of the same questions are asked in order to get an idea of the cost of cremation. Funeral directors look at three categories of cremation:

Cremation without services is called a direct cremation. In this case, we file the paperwork, take care of the body, bring it to the crematory, make sure the ashes get back to the family, and provide the documentation. Because the amount of cash advances is less in this situation, the bulk of the funeral expenses will be in funeral service fees. We do very few of these services, but these range anywhere between $1,400 and $2,900.

Cremation with services is when a cremation takes place before the memorial service and visitation; therefore, it doesn't require embalming or a casket. That can be anywhere between $3,700 and $5,500.

More traditional cremation services are when the body is embalmed and placed into a ceremonial casket for the visitation, then brought to the church or location of the funeral service. The cremation takes place after that. Because it requires embalming and the use of the ceremonial casket in addition to an urn, it is usually more costly than the other two options. This can range in price between $6,000 and $8,000.

There are definitely benefits to having a more traditional service. If you recall from Question 12 where we discussed the benefits of the public viewing (or visitation), by choosing to allow extended family and friends to see the deceased, you offer them an opportunity to confront the reality of this death and help them to move forward.

QUESTION THIRTY

WHAT ARE THE DEATH BENEFITS FOR VETERANS?

If you are a veteran, you may be entitled to several different benefits. One is the veteran's life insurance benefit that is offered to every serviceman and servicewoman. Every veteran was discharged with the ability to keep that insurance (usually $10,000 to $20,000) in place, but very few veterans choose to keep it. When you're discharged out of the service at age 21, the last thing you really want to be thinking about is the possibility of paying for life insurance, especially when you think your life is going to go on forever. However, veteran's life insurance is one of the cheapest forms of life insurance available. If you let it go, you let it go. But if you have it, keep it. It's very inexpensive life insurance.

Veterans who are honorably discharged are entitled to these burial benefits:
- A flag (the funeral director will get this for the veteran's survivors)
- An honor squad of active duty military personnel that will present the flag at the grave (this must be requested in

71

advance and is a benefit that a lot of people are not aware of and sadly don't take advantage of)

- A presidential memorial certificate signed by the current president to show the nation's appreciation for the veteran's service
- Burial benefits of $300 or more, depending on where the veteran might have died, whether there was a VA benefit because of a service-associated disability, or some other VA benefit (The funeral director should fill out the burial benefits application and file it on behalf of the family. Not all veterans are entitled to a payment but one should always apply for it. Within about six weeks, the VA will send a letter that says whether the request was approved or denied and the reasons why.)
- A grave space in the national cemetery of their choice is available to all honorably discharged veterans, as well as a space for their surviving spouse and/or dependent child (Currently the national cemeteries require a minimum enclosure [like an open-bottom vault] for the casket. They will provide you with one, but if you wish, you can choose to buy a more protective vault from the funeral home. If you do that, the VA will reimburse you for the amount they would've paid for their minimum enclosure.)
- A marker or an emblem for an existing marker at the grave space in either the national or a private cemetery (in private cemeteries, only the veteran is entitled to a VA-paid marker)

Veterans' benefits are subject to change, and you can usually talk to your funeral director for current information about these benefits. You can also go to www.cem.va.gov to get more information online.

QUESTION THIRTY-ONE

HOW CAN I SAVE MONEY?

The best way to save money, assuming you have done all of the things to choose the right cremation and funeral provider, are to be honest with the funeral director and say, "I have a limited amount of funds. What can you do to help me make this meaningful, but cut down on the price?" I get that quite a bit, and I'm very grateful when a family is that honest with me.

Everybody is afraid of emotional overspending, but the truth is that I really don't see this. Most families come in with other family members or friends, so people who are thinking very clearly and using level heads surround them. In addition to that, the funeral director, if they work up to their reputation, will be very levelheaded about helping you as well.

There many ways that we can cut costs, including:
- Consider the casket and vault. Are you willing to use something of lesser quality or lesser price? The truth is, all caskets do the same thing, and in many cases, people cannot tell the difference between an expensive casket and an inexpensive one.

73

- Consider the flowers that the family is buying. Many options exist that can limit this expense, including flowering plants that are available at your local greenhouse.
- Consider the obituary expense. In my marketplace, obituaries are very expensive, so we usually try to limit the content to the survivors and funeral services. That's the information that people look for most.
- Consider the funeral home services. Are there any services or automotive equipment that we could cut out? Alternatively, is there a way that the funeral director would just reach an accommodation with the family? Most of the time, if you're honest with them, the funeral home will return the favor and help accommodate whatever funds you have available for the services.

You should never be embarrassed about being on a budget. The funeral director knows that it's a tough economy. Recently, I've been helping to transition people to less expensive funerals while keeping a similar type of service.

We have different options for caskets now that are less expensive than we've had in the past. They might involve bringing them in from overseas, but they can be dramatically less expensive than domestically produced caskets.

Wood caskets, in the past, used to be made of solid species wood. Now, like most furniture, we're making caskets out of veneer. Veneer is a thin covering over a wood substrate. This can cut the cost of a casket dramatically, but still keep the beautiful appearance of a wood casket. (But of course, we still do carry domestically produced, solid wood caskets.)

Your funeral director will help you, but remember that you have all the power in this equation. Even if the death has taken place and the funeral director has brought the body to their funeral home and some work has been done, you are not obligated to finish the arrangements with them. If you feel uncomfortable, or if you feel you're being manipulated into spending too much, you always have the right to get up, walk out, and choose another provider.

Section Seven

Death and Red Tape

QUESTION THIRTY-TWO

CAN MY IDENTITY BE STOLEN AT DEATH?

Yes. I know that's not the answer you want to hear, but that is the reality. Some years ago in Indiana, a group of thieves would call people who recently had a death in their family. They presented themselves as representatives of the state health department and needed the date of birth and Social Security number in order to file the death certificate. That seemed legitimate enough, and so many people gave them what they wanted. With the combination of name, date of birth, and Social Security number, you can pretty much steal anybody's identity, and you don't have to be in this country to do it.

Identity theft is on the rise, and thieves are opportunists, so they will look for any vulnerability they can. We take steps, and all funeral homes should do this, to protect the decedent's identity. As soon as we get the Social Security number from the family, we electronically notify the Social Security Administration so that they are aware that this person has died. Does this eliminate the threat of identity theft? No, but it greatly limits the possibility of it. Additionally, our files are confidential and not shared with anyone else. Lastly, the people who work here all pass a stringent

76

background check and can absolutely be trusted.

Now, what can you do to protect a person's identity at the time of death? Usually, at the time of death, a lot of health records have accumulated. There may not be a need to hold onto to these health records, and if that's the case, then bundle them all up, bring them to the bank, and put them in your bank's shred box, which they will most likely do free of charge. Or shred everything at home. Do not burn it, do not tear it up. It has been proven that thieves can reconstitute images from ashes. When filing estate issues, make sure that any forms that you don't fully complete, are shredded as well.

Online applications, although convenient, may give you some concern. Never fill out a form with sensitive information on a public computer, like the ones at the library. If you don't feel comfortable submitting something over the internet, offer to download the form and send it via certified mail.

If you're filing a life insurance claim, life insurance agents from that company are available to help you do that work. Call them, and when they come to your house, or when you visit with them, make sure that you see the proper credentials.

If ever you get a request for any personal information over the phone, via text, or through your computer, be extremely cautious.

Verify a website's address. Does it look correct? Anything sent to you from your bank, let's call it "AmeriBank," will almost surely come from AmeriBank.com, and not .net, .ca, or .org. The company's name only followed by .com is more likely to be legitimate. However, criminals are tricky; something like AmeriBankCorp.com looks very legitimate, but can be hiding a scam.

If you are ever asked for personal information over the phone, ask for a number to call them back. If they won't give you one, the conversation should be over. If it's someone supposedly calling from your bank, or the social security office, those phone numbers are readily available on the Internet, on the back of credit cards, or in the phone book. Call one of those numbers to see if there is any issue with your account.

Text messages can also seem very legitimate and often appear to come from your bank. They may warn you about an issue with your account and give you a phone number to call. Do not call that number. Just calling an unfamiliar number back can open you up to getting fees charged to your phone bill. If you're concerned about a text that appears to be from your bank, do not call the number that came with the text, rather call your bank's customer service phone number that is usually on your statement or on the bank's website.

QUESTION THIRTY-THREE

HOW DO I BEGIN TO HANDLE THE ESTATE?

The first thing that most people do after a death is to file for life insurance. Life insurance is usually not part of the estate and can be applied for immediately. All that you need in order to file for the life insurance is a copy of the policy, the claim form, and the death certificate. Most life insurance companies settle the claim very, very quickly, usually within three weeks after the death.

Other estate matters fall into the categories of real estate, titled property, and personal effects.

Real estate involves the change of a title or the sale of real estate. If a married couple owned a house and one spouse survives, there is no need to change that title immediately. In most cases you can leave it be until the surviving spouse dies or the property is sold. Only then will you need death certificates from all involved in order to finalize the process.

If property is owned by a single person, and that person dies, then the executor or, in our state, the personal representative needs to file for that within the estate. A personal representative is named in the will as somebody who has the authority granted by the deceased to handle that estate. Cars, boats, and planes, those things with a title, are easily transferred with a copy of the death certificate, a personal representative, and a trip to the motor vehicle department.

Personal bank accounts are a little more difficult because banks now require a lot of paperwork in order to close those accounts. This usually requires a personal representative, the copy of the death certificate, and a lot of patience.

It's worth noting the very common misconception that the power of attorney is a power that exists for as long as you need it. It is not. That power ends at death. Power of attorney serves a very important function while a compromised person is still alive. It is granted to allow a person to stand in the compromised person's shoes and make decisions for them, but that decision-making power always ends at death. Many people don't realize that this is the case. In short, the person who holds the power of attorney is not automatically the personal representative after the death.

QUESTION THIRTY-FOUR

DO I NEED AN ATTORNEY?

Most people don't want to pay for an attorney. That's not unusual; that's almost universal. But the truth is that an attorney can save you a lot of time and hassle.

Most wills can be done simply and for about $500, and in doing so, they really take care of a lot of things, not just those regarding the estate at the time of death, but the more likely situation when people outlive their assets.

An attorney can give you guidance specific to your situation, and they can help take the guesswork out of planning your estate. It is always a good idea to have your estate in order, so that if you should die unexpectedly, you know that your assets will be used in the way you would have wanted.

Do you need an attorney? If you've asked that question, you probably do.

Section Eight

How to Prepare

QUESTION THIRTY-FIVE

WHAT ARE THE ADVANTAGES OF PRE-PLANNING?

Planning your own funeral is something that most people don't like to think about. Pre-arrangement allows you to make your final arrangements at your own pace, at a time when you feel calm, healthy, and rational.

You can pre-arrange your funeral using online resources such as our secure PreArrange Online network at www.MuellerMemorial.com by clicking the Funeral Planning tab or you can just contact a trusted funeral home. You can also pre-arrange the funeral of a loved one.

Many people wait too long to start this process. Putting it off until a death takes place adds additional emotional stress and forces your family to guess what you might have liked. Honestly, more and more people are planning their own services because they are not sure that their family will do anything at their death.

A funeral home will sit down with you, at no obligation, and give you a very accurate estimate of what the cost would be in today's dollars, so that you can plan accordingly. Planning can be as simple as responding to this checklist:

- Prepare a list of people who should be contacted in case of a medical emergency or death
- Write an obituary or write down information needed for an obituary
- Decide where the obituary should appear
- Choose the type of service you would like (burial or cremation)
- Choose the details of your service:
- Cemetery lot location
- Casket type/cremation urn type
- Vault/sectional crypt
- Religious, military, other type of service
- Your pallbearers
- Your music selection
- Your flowers
- Readings at service and who will read them
- Clothes and jewelry to be worn
- Choose the charity, church, or organization you would like donations to be made to
- Choose your funeral and visitation location

As I mentioned before, funeral services are becoming very personalized. Now, while you have the time to think about what you really want and the time to get creative, why not get very specific about every aspect? You might decide to:

- Pick out the photos you want in your video montage
- Make a note on your religious beliefs
- Specify the place people should meet up after your service
- Select the tunes you want played on a jukebox
- Demand that everyone wear your favorite color
- Specify the kinds of flowers you like (or don't like)
- Make up a signature cocktail to be served
- Write down all of your favorite things in life
- Pick the people you want to eulogize you
- Make a list of your favorite causes
- Write personal messages to those closest to you

The more specific you get, the more meaningful your memorial will be. I remember one family we served where the father of two young girls was terminally ill. Over time, I came to find out that while he was sick he realized that he wasn't going to be around for the major events in his girls' lives. So, before he died, he wrote both his daughters cards of congratulations that were given to them on their graduation and wedding days. A little forethought can be a powerful force in creating your legacy.

QUESTION THIRTY-SIX

HOW DO I KNOW MY WISHES WILL BE FOLLOWED?

Legally, I'm speaking of the state of Minnesota, but most states would honor this as well. If I have written instructions from the decedent that states what should be done at the funeral, then I am obligated, and the family is obligated, to follow those instructions.

So if you have something specific that you'd like done at the time of your death, put it into writing. Get a date on it, have a witness to it, and ideally, put it in the funeral home's file. Do not put it in your safe deposit box. Safe deposit boxes usually cannot be accessed until long after the death, and by then the services are finished.

We have an older gentleman who comes in every once in a while just to chat and check up on his file and make sure that he still likes the picture he's chosen and that the obituary is up to date. He also likes to update who's in and who's out for pallbearers this week.

In lieu of visiting your funeral home, you can create a list of the people you do (and do not) want involved in planning your funeral. Let these people know that they have been assigned this position, and give them all copies of your written wishes. In this way, if something does happen to you, there will be multiple people who know exactly what you want done.

QUESTION THIRTY-SEVEN

CAN I PREPAY FOR MY FUNERAL?

Yes, you can. Most states allow money to be put into a funeral trust or into funeral insurance for funding the funeral. It is important to know which vehicle is going to be used for funding because you'll want the peace of mind in knowing exactly how and where your money will be placed.

Some states, like mine, are very consumer oriented. In my state of Minnesota, 100 percent of the money, plus all of the interest, must stay in the funeral trust account for the purpose of the funeral. If it is funded by an insurance policy, which is generally the case, then that insurance is there strictly to pay for the funeral at the time of death. Policies used for funeral purposes do not have a loan value.

Some states allow the funeral director to take the interest that the account earns every year, or even allow the funeral director to take the interest plus a portion of the principal. If this is the case, do not put your money with them. Make sure that your policy is gaining interest and that it's going to your account. You want to be certain that all of that money is being used for the benefit of your funeral, including interest or dividends.

If you've taken the time to pre-arrange, then it makes sense to prefund your funeral. Telling people what you want may be a moot point if there are no funds to bring your plans to fruition.

Furthermore, there are elements of prefunding that can serve as asset protection, but we'll get to that shortly.

QUESTION THIRTY-EIGHT

IF I GET ESTIMATES AND PREPAY, ARE THE COSTS FROZEN?

Some funeral homes may guarantee that the amount in the account will be sufficient to take care of the expense at the time of death, although I don't understand how that makes good business sense, and I don't think that's a good thing for you in the long run.

The truth is that most trust accounts now pay interest in the range of less-than-one-percent. Dividends on insurance policies are currently paying 2.4 percent while the inflation rate is 4.5 percent.

If our expenses go up at the rate of 4.5 percent per year, and the amount that was funded for a funeral gains interest at the rate of 2.4 percent per year, then the fund will never catch up with prices. Cost freezing is a bad business decision made by a questionable funeral home. I would not make a deal with them. I would go to somebody who says he or she will make every effort to try to provide these services at the time, but you may want to add a little bit more money into the account as an inflation contingency. In the event that there is more money in the policy than the cost of the funeral, the overage is refunded to the family.

Insist on these safeguards. It is a smart and prudent thing to do for your family.

QUESTION THIRTY-NINE

WHAT IF I OUTLIVE MY ASSETS?

Outliving one's assets is a very common concern whenever somebody is prearranging their funeral. The truth is that financial planners look at the possibility of building wealth, and life insurance companies look at transferring wealth to the next generation. But what financial planners and insurance companies often don't anticipate is the possibility that a person will require long-term care and outlive their assets.

This is a reality of our future. I can't tell you how many people I know who did not plan for this possibility and are now forced, because of a spend-down, to cash out their common life insurance policy, which they had intended to use to pay for their funeral expenses.

If you enter into long-term care, there is a chance that you'll be subject to a spend-down of all your assets before Medical Assistance (MA) will begin to contribute. Cashing in your common life insurance policies is part of that spend-down.

The good news is that in some states like Minnesota, you can set up a specific type of irrevocable trust with a funeral home and that money, or most commonly a funded insurance policy, is not counted toward your assets. It is also exempt from the five-year look-back. This way you can have the memorial that you want without affecting your eligibility for assistance.

Laws regarding MA vary from state to state and change frequently, but prearranging and prepaying for a funeral is one way that you can segregate funds from your estate. This way you can use the funds plus the dividends to pay for your funeral and keep it out of the reach of the government.

A good funeral home can help you sort out what options are best for you and your family without a fee. For the most current information go to www.MuellerMemorial.com and click the Funeral Planning tab.

BRINGING IT HOME

So there it is; some of the most commonly asked questions of a funeral director, updated for what's going on in today's world.

I mentioned earlier that the Federal Trade Commission passed a rule regarding funeral directors in 1983. One of the best things that came out of the FTC rule is that it obligates a funeral director to give you the information you want over the phone, without requiring you to come in and without requiring you to divulge who you are or what your intentions are. Most funeral directors are very willing to do this. If they are not, you should not choose them. I bring this up because the FTC rule has ensured consumer access to funeral information, and I want you to fully use that information and do your research when choosing a funeral home.

Most people look at the planning a funeral as an ordeal. And it can be. But I can tell you that if you don't plan for it, if you don't do anything to prepare, if you don't make your wishes known, it will be much more of an unnecessary burden to your family than it might have been.

Whether your funeral planning needs are imminent or far in the future, it is important to have a guide. A funeral director can be your guide, and they can do it at no expense to you. That initial consultation and several follow-ups can be had at no cost to you. They're happy to help you get what you want.

Mortality is a serious topic and one that is difficult for many to address. I appreciate you taking the time to help yourself and your family deal with a subject that every person will have to address one way or another.

The final thought I'll leave you with is, don't wait! You really never know when having your wishes known will be needed. So, don't make this one of the things that you will get around to someday. In its simplest form, making your wishes known can take just a couple of minutes of jotting things down. Do that if you don't have the time to meet with a funeral director. But if you make the time to plan this out, you could have one amazing memorial!

Still have questions or want to get started planning? You can contact the author at Mueller Memorial in St. Paul or White Bear Lake. Just call 651-774-9797 or email Scott at Info@MuellerMemorial.com.

ABOUT THE AUTHOR

One of nine kids, Scott Mueller was the only of his siblings to find a career in his family's funeral business. At age sixteen, Scott went to work with his dad, Al, at the Mueller Funeral Homes and has been a licensed Funeral Director since 1980.

During his career he has worked nationally to train other funeral directors in service and operational best practices. He has served as President of the National Association of Approved Morticians, as a board member of the HealthEast Foundation, and as the Chair of the White Bear Area Chamber of Commerce, among other community involvement.

Scott lives with his wife, Heidi, in White Bear Lake, Minnesota, and enjoys spending time with his family—especially his three adorable grandchildren.

Made in the USA
Lexington, KY
23 August 2019